Kissably Cute!

How many little princes do you have in your family? Keep track of their all-too-fast leaps from tiny tadpoles to young men of the world. (You can use the photos to embarrass him when he's a teen!)

Special Supplies: Papers - Cardstock (Black, White & Red), Keeping Memories Alive (Green check); Font - CK Expedition on Creating Keepsakes Vol. 1 CD; 5/8" circle punch (pupils), 1/4" circle punch (cheeks and toes).

Use a 1/4" circle punch to make 12 toe tips. Glue each in place.

Kissably Cute! patterns

A Very 'Buzzy' Year! patterns

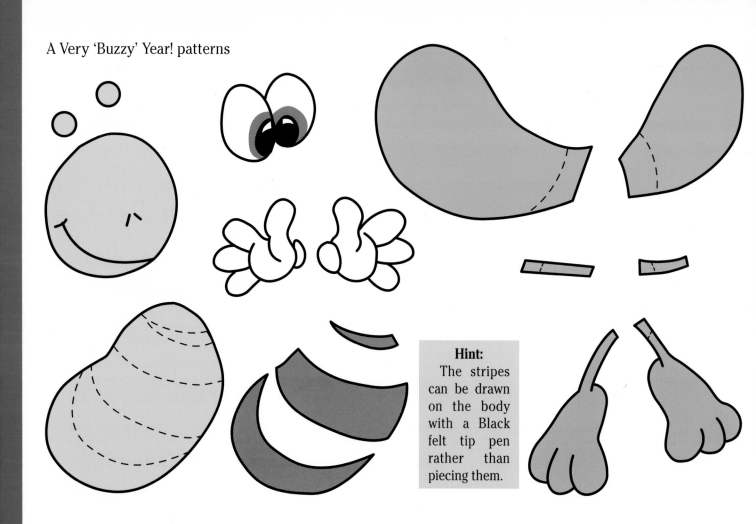

Hint:
The stripes can be drawn on the body with a Black felt tip pen rather than piecing them.

Just Fluttering by... patterns

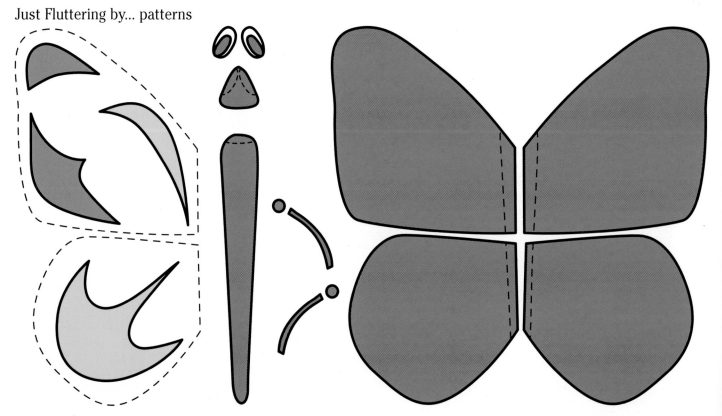

A Very 'Buzzy' Year!

Any mother knows that every minute of a child's life is a very busy one! Make sure to catch that funny face that he loves - and you can't stand! The picture will be priceless in the years to come! To both of you!

Special Supplies: Papers - Cardstock (White, Yellow, Black, Green, Tan & Blue); Font - CK Contemporary Caps on Creating Keepsakes Wedding CD; Provo Craft grass scissors; 3/4" oval punch (eyes); 1/4" circle punch (antennae).

Bee Happy!

Just Fluttering by...

'Light as the air and pretty as a flower' - a good description of what a child sees! Everything is new and fascinating! Keep track of those expressions of awe and wonder with photos!

Special Supplies: Papers - Cardstock (Blue, Yellow, Black, Yellow, White & solid Purple), Making Memories (Purple dot); Font - CK Hearts on Creating Keepsakes Wedding CD; 1/4" oval punch (eyes); 1/8" oval punch (pupils); 1/8" circle punch (antennae).

Butterfly

Kimberly

Kimberly loves bright colorful toys, puppies, kittens and butterflies!

A Den of Dandy Lions! patterns

Classic Black & White! patterns

A Den of Dandy Lions!

A group of lions is called a 'pride.' What's there to be more proud of than a group of wriggling, giggling kids! Keep track of all those childhood friends and antics before the bunch of them grows into strapping young adults! Click to it! Time's a-wasting!

Special Supplies: Papers - Cardstock (Black, Gold, Orange & Black), Provo Craft (Plaid); Font - Dom Casual, free from fortunecity.com/sky-scraper/integer/317/; $1/2$" oval punch (eyes, eyelids); $1/4$" circle punch (pupils).

A Roaring Good Time

Janna and Seth love to ride in the park and visit the animals in the ZOO.

This place is a zoo

Classic Black & White!

Who says all photos have to be in color! Sometimes the time's just right for a simple black and white shot! Place your child's photo along with one of Granddad or Grandmother at the same age on the same page! Everyone will be delighted with the mix!

Special Supplies: Papers - Cardstock (Red, Gold, Black & White), Frances Meyer (Zebra print); Font - Ck Voluptuous on Creating Keepsakes Wedding CD; $1/4$" oval punch (eye).

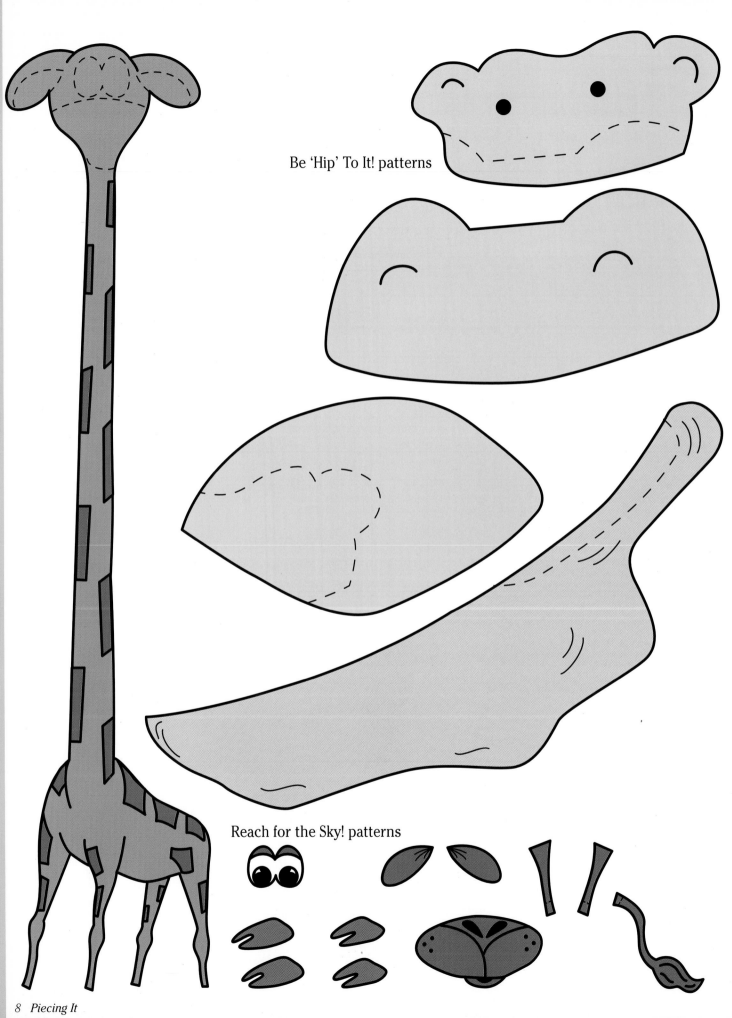

Be 'Hip' To It! patterns

Reach for the Sky! patterns

Reach for the Sky!

How tall will that toddler grow to be? Track those spurts of growth - other than adding up the bills for clothes, that is! On each birthday take a picture of the little one standing in front of a doorway or refrigerator. If they reach the top before they're 12, sign them up for basketball!

Special Supplies: Papers - Cardstock (Maroon, White & Black); Keeping Memories Alive (Red check); Font - Comix Heavy, free from fortunecity.com/skyscraper/integer/317; $3/8$" oval punch (eyes); $1/4$" circle punch (pupils).

STRETCHING TO NEW HEIGHTS

What better way to celebrate!

Hip Hippo

Hooray!

Be 'Hip' to It!

Sure, there are days when anyone would love to loll in a big ol' pond. Days like that are few and far between, though! Keep track of a great achievement by a friend, a family member or a coworker and make them a page to remember it by!

Special Supplies: Papers - Cardstock (Black, Grey & White); Font: Ck Chunky Block on Creating Keepsakes Baby CD; $1/8$" circle punch (eyes), $1^1/4$", $5/8$" and $3/8$" swirl punches; Pink chalk (for shading body).

Squeek Up! patterns

You're No Dumbo! patterns

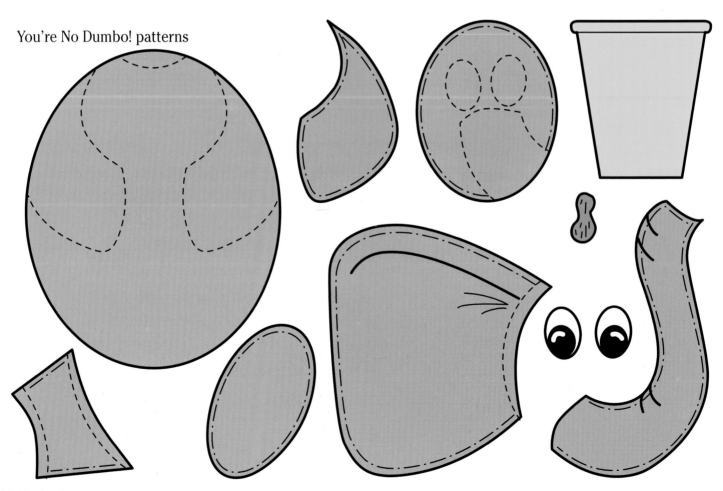

Say Cheese

Squeek Up!

How do you feel about that zoo trip? How about the camping trip when Dad forgot the tent - and it rained! What about that first school play? Put those memories into photo form to save the laughs, smiles - and groans - that went with the day!

Special Supplies: Papers - Cardstock (Brown, Gold, Dark Gray, Pink, White & Black), Provo Craft (Gray swirl); 1/2" circle punch (nose), 1/4" circle punch (pupils); Dark Gray chalk (for shading body); Gold chalk (for shading cheese).

You're No Dumbo!

Take them to the circus! Buy them some popcorn and cotton candy! Take a picture of them as they 'ooh!' at the lions and laugh at the clowns! Make it a day of fun and fairways to be remembered forever and ever!

Special Supplies: Papers - Cardstock (Gray, Dark Gray, White, Brown & Yellow), Provo Craft (Blue check) and Keeping Memories Alive (Yellow check); 1/2" oval punch (nose), 5/8" sun punch (hair).

BUCKETS AND BUCKETS OF FUN

NUTS

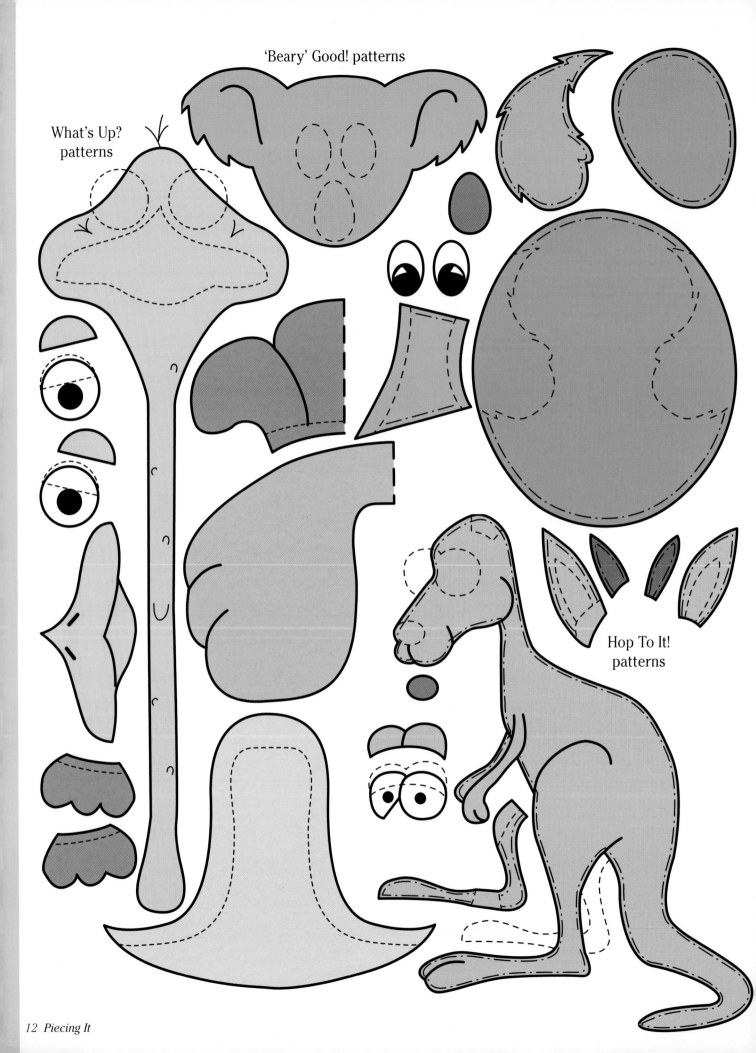

'Beary' Good! patterns

What's Up? patterns

Hop To It! patterns

What's Up?!

What is that? A bird? A plane? No! It's a memory! Take a picture!

Special Supplies: Paper - Cardstock (White & Black), Provo Craft (Dark Blue, Gray swirl & Gray check), Keeping Memories Alive (Pink) and Paper Patch (Yellow); 1/2" circle punch (eyes), 1/4" circle punch (pupils).

BEARY BEST BUDS

Zac and Nate - on the rocks!

G'day Mate

'Beary' Good!

What a great smile you have!

Special Supplies: Papers - Cardstock (Light Tan, Green, Brown & Tan) and Provo Craft (Floral print); Font - Ck Fill In on Creating Keepsakes Vol. 1 CD; 5/8" oval punch (eyes); 1/4" circle punch (pupils); 5/8" oval punch (nose).

Hop To It!

Capture an adventure on film!

Special Supplies: Papers - Cardstock (Brown, Beige,Tan, White & Black) and Paper Patch (Brown plaid); Font - Christie from Printshop; 1/8" circle punch (pupils).

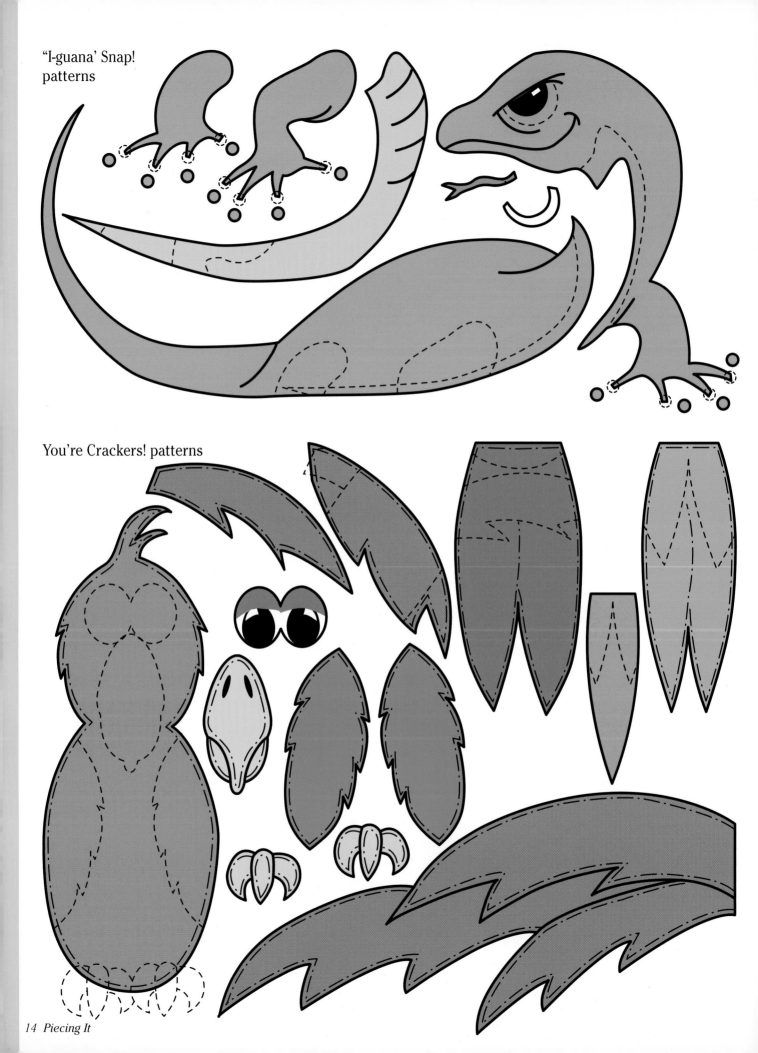

"I-guana' Snap! patterns

You're Crackers! patterns

'I-guana' Snap!

Smile! Even when you find all kinds of creepy crawling critters in the pockets of the laundry! Just remember, one day <u>your</u> kids will have <u>their</u> own kids - who'll be just like <u>them</u>! With any luck! Just be sure you have pictures to back up your stories!

Special Supplies: Papers - Cardstock (Orange, Black, Gold, White & Red) and Paper Patch (Patterned); Font - Wacko, free from fontmaster.com; $1/8$" circle punch (toes); Orange chalk (for body shading).

You're Crackers!

Every day is different, so keep track of the 'nutso' days along with the not-so-grand days! You'll be glad you did! If the kids think you are a little camera-crazy, that's okay! It's rare to catch them in their finest plumage - while they're still clean!

Special Supplies: Papers - Cardstock (Blue, White, Turquoise, Orange, Gold White & Green); Blue chalk (to create the 'clouds' on the White background paper.

Bandit of Hearts! patterns

Hooked on Fun! patterns

Eager Beavers! patterns

Eager Beavers!

No matter how small the task or activity, make sure to have a record of your child's progress!

Special Supplies: Papers - Cardstock (Green, Brown, Black, White & Gold), Keeping Memories Alive (Brown plaid); Font - Corel with hand-drawn leaves; 1/8" oval punch (pupils); Dark Brown chalk (for shading body).

Busy as a Beaver

Catch of the day

Bandit of Hearts

Ricky Raccoon washes his food in water before he eats.

Hooked on Fun!

How big was that fish - really!?!

Special Supplies: Papers - Cardstock (White, Yellow & Black), Provo (Olive), Keeping Memories Alive (Dark Green print); Font - Jester, free from fontmaster.com; 1/4" circle punch (for eyes), 1/8" circle punch (for pupils) 1/4" oval punch (for chain holes).

Bandit of Hearts!

Catch them in the act!

Special Supplies: Papers - Cardstock (Beige, Tan, Dark Green & Black), Paper Patch (Green plaid); 1/8" oval punch (for pupils), 1/2" oval punch (for nose); Brown chalk (for shading body); Fiskars Victorian Rotary Blade (for border).

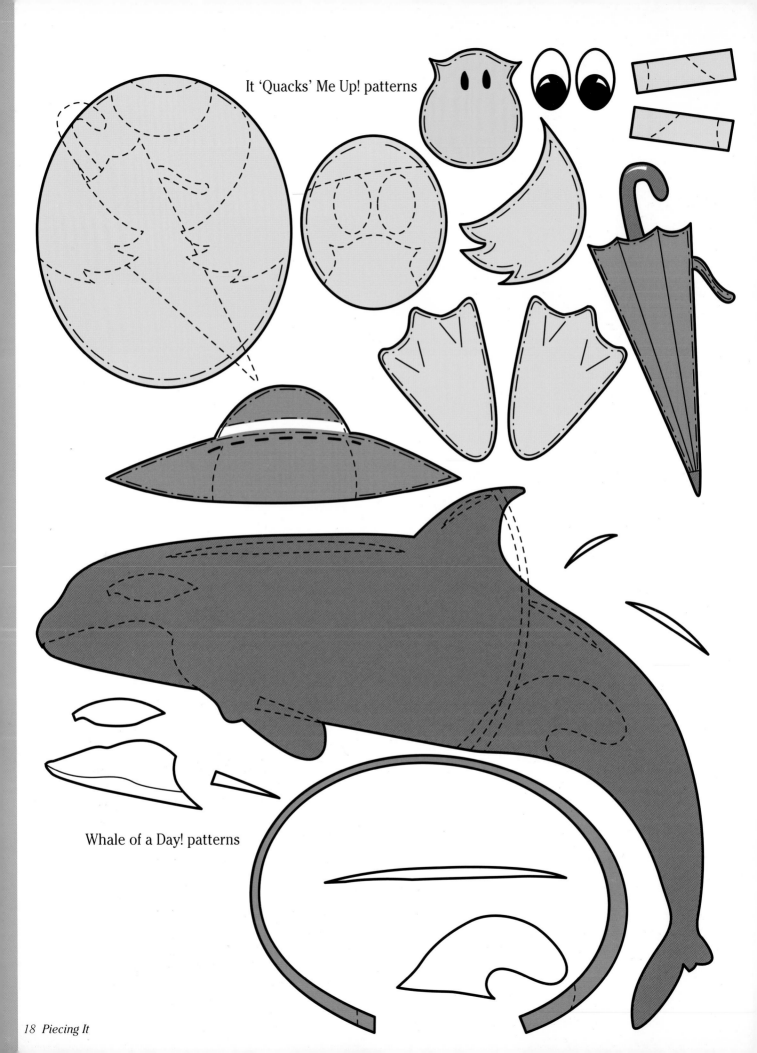

It 'Quacks' Me Up! patterns

Whale of a Day! patterns

It 'Quacks' Me Up!

Oh, look! They are just ducky when they smile that way! And look at the awe the bubbles inspire! Such moments deserve a unique page in a very special book of memories!

Special Supplies: Papers - Cardstock (Yellow & White), Paper Patch (Blue plaid and Red heart print) and Keeping Memories Alive (Yellow check); $5/8$" oval punch (eyes); $3/4$" star punch (sun).

Whale of a Day!

Remember how wet we got when the whale hit the water right in front of us? That day at the aquarium show was flooded with fun! We laughed and dripped all the way back to the car!

Special Supplies: Papers - Cardstock (Black, White & Red) and Paper Patch (Red print).

Super Bowl Story! patterns

Pictures With A
Real 'Porpoise!
patterns

Super Bowl Story!

Even though he can't fetch or roll over, we all love that cute little fish - our first family pet! Dad loved setting up the bowl so much that he got a tropical fish screen saver for his computer! Long live the memory of 'Bubbles!'

Special Supplies: Papers - Cardstock (Lime Green, Yellow, White Black & Peach) and Paper Adventures (Water print); Font - Underwater. free from fontfreak.com; $1/2$" circle punch (eye), Gray chalk (fin shading); Green chalk (for shading seaweed); Orange chalk (for shading starfish).

Pictures With a Real 'Porpoise!

Remember when we couldn't wait for an afternoon shower to play in the puddles?

Great photos remind us of life's simple pleasures in a way that will last forever.

Special Supplies: Papers - Cardstock (Yellow, Blue, Dark Gray, Light Gray & Light Blue) and Frances Meyer (Plaid); Font - Doodle Outline from Page Printables CD; $1/8$" circle punch (eye).

What a Big 'Crock' of
Fun! patterns

Life Is A Snap!
patterns

What a Big 'Crock' of Fun!

That school trip to the River Conservation Farm was a day of fun and learning! We saw all sorts of new things - from the animals to the air boats that float so-o-o-o fast on top of the water! We were floating in memories and giggles all the way home!

Special Supplies: Papers - Cardstock (Blue, Green, Yellow & White) and Frances Meyer (Striped); Font - CK Crooked Classes on Creating Keepsakes Wedding CD; Provo Craft Grass Scissors; 1/2" circle punch (eyes, eyelids), 1/8" circle punch (pupils); Provo Craft fly sticker; Orange chalk (for shading underbelly).

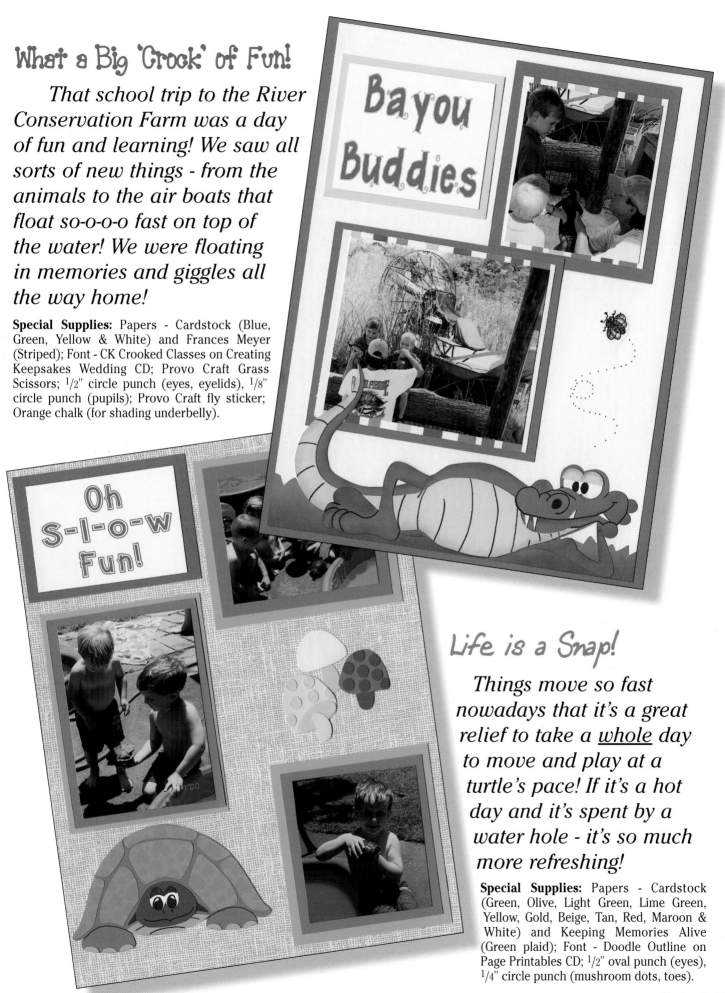

Life is a Snap!

Things move so fast nowadays that it's a great relief to take a <u>whole</u> day to move and play at a turtle's pace! If it's a hot day and it's spent by a water hole - it's so much more refreshing!

Special Supplies: Papers - Cardstock (Green, Olive, Light Green, Lime Green, Yellow, Gold, Beige, Tan, Red, Maroon & White) and Keeping Memories Alive (Green plaid); Font - Doodle Outline on Page Printables CD; 1/2" oval punch (eyes), 1/4" circle punch (mushroom dots, toes).

Hop To It! patterns

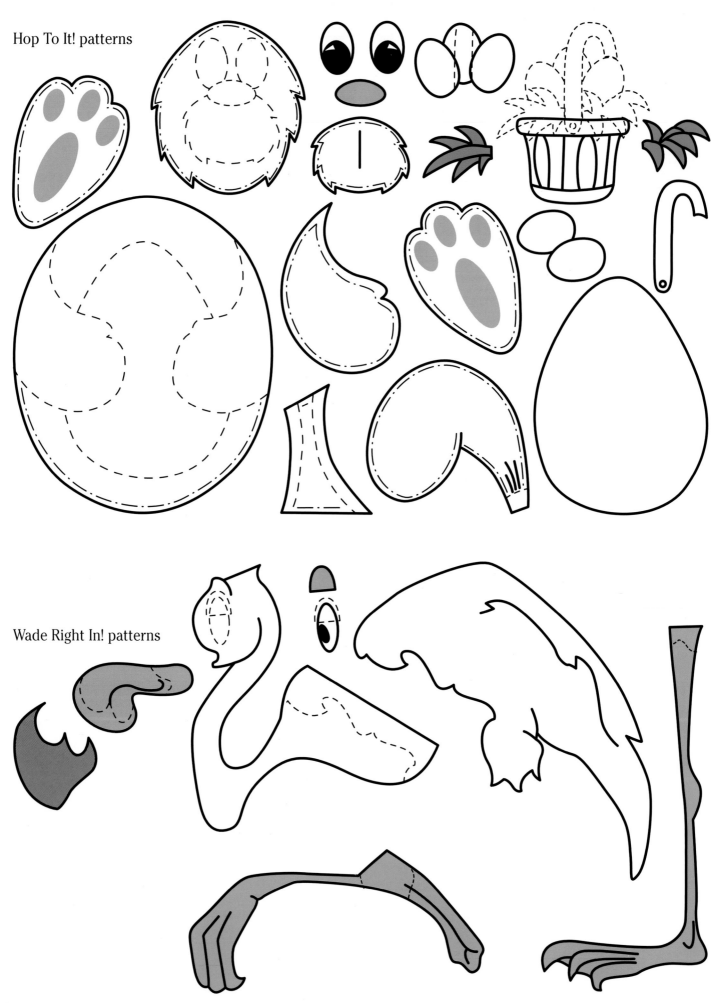

Wade Right In! patterns

Wade Right In!

If you wait until everyone is primped and posed just right, you are going to have a really skinny scrapbook! Go ahead! Snap that picture! Sometimes a spontaneous pose is the best pose to catch! How else could you have gotten that shot of Uncle Jim with the Christmas bow stuck on his bald head?

Special Supplies: Paper - Cardstock (Pink, Blue, Hot Pink, White & Black) and Sonburn (Plaid); 1/2" oval punch (eye).

Hop To It!

Their first Easter egg hunt! Their first chocolate bunny! Her first Easter dress - complete with patent leather Mary Janes and a frilly little hat! His first long-legged Easter suit! He looked so cute with that new tie! The firsts are fine photo fare!

Special Supplies: Papers - Cardstock (Blue, Pink & White) and Sonburn (Tie-dyed); 1/2" oval punch (eyes).

Get Moo-ving!
patterns

Pony Up A Pose! patterns

GOT MILK?

Get Moo-ving!

Have you ever been to a farm and milked a cow? That's some funny business! Did you take a picture? Or maybe it was the kids' first attempt to make cookies! Get a record of the kitchen disaster so everyone can laugh about it later! Maybe the baby took its first swig from a glass! That's a once-in-a-lifetime shot!

Special Supplies: Papers - Cardstock (Hot Pink, White & Black) and Paper Patch (Black check); Font: MooCow, free from fontmaster.com; AccuCut Die Cut (grass).

Pony Up a Pose!

Come on, everyone! Get closer together and look at me! Smile! This picture of the leaf pile destruction is a delight! Or maybe you can get four generations of the family to sit still long enough to make a wonderful memory!

Special Supplies: Papers - Cardstock (Beige, Brown, White & Black), Paper Adventures (velveteen) and Provo Craft (frame and border); Font: CK Chunky Block on the Creating Keepsakes Baby CD; 1/4" circle punch (eye), 1/8" circle punch (pupils).

Just Be - 'Caws'! patterns

Lay It On Me! patterns

Just Be - 'Caws'!

Who is that cute young actor playing the pirate in the school play? Get several pictures of the young thespian-in-training! What about the awards ceremony in the third grade? And that spelling bee ribbon! Every day is a prize!

Special Supplies: Papers - Cardstock (Maroon, Black, Gold, Blue, Green & White) and Provo Craft (Red pattern); Font: Ck Flower Power on Creating Keepsakes Baby CD; 1" circle punch (ribbon top), 5/8" flower punch; Fiskars Victorian rotary blade (border).

Lay It On Me!

How did you get that shot of Katie with the finger-paint on her face? Sometimes a good photo is the result of a sneaky - and very quiet - camera operator! Practice your stealth and catch a wealth of great moments!

Special Supplies: Papers - Cardstock (Yellow, Red & White) and Paper Patch (Red heart and Red polka dot); Font: Dancin Let, free from terrashare.com; 1/2" oval punch (eyes).

'Hot Diggity Dawg!
patterns

Stuffed With Fun! patterns

Hot Diggity Dawg!

Be in just the right place at just the right time with your loaded camera and look at the amazing results! A good picture can improve any occasion - a lot!

Special Supplies: Papers - Cardstock (Dark Brown, Tan, Maroon, Light Red, White & Black) and Paper Patch (Plaid); Font: TnC Scraps design; 1/2" circle punch (nose), 1/4" circle punch (pupils).

Stuffed with Fun!

Daniel's tummy is full of yummy turkey. Time for an afternoon nap amid all the hubbub of Thanksgiving Day. He needs to rest up for play time later.

And then there's the traditional touch football game out back!

Special Supplies: Papers - Cardstock (Maroon, Beige, Dark Brown, Medium Brown, Tan & Reddish Brown) and Sonburn (Leaf print); Font: Signboard, free from abstractfonts.com.

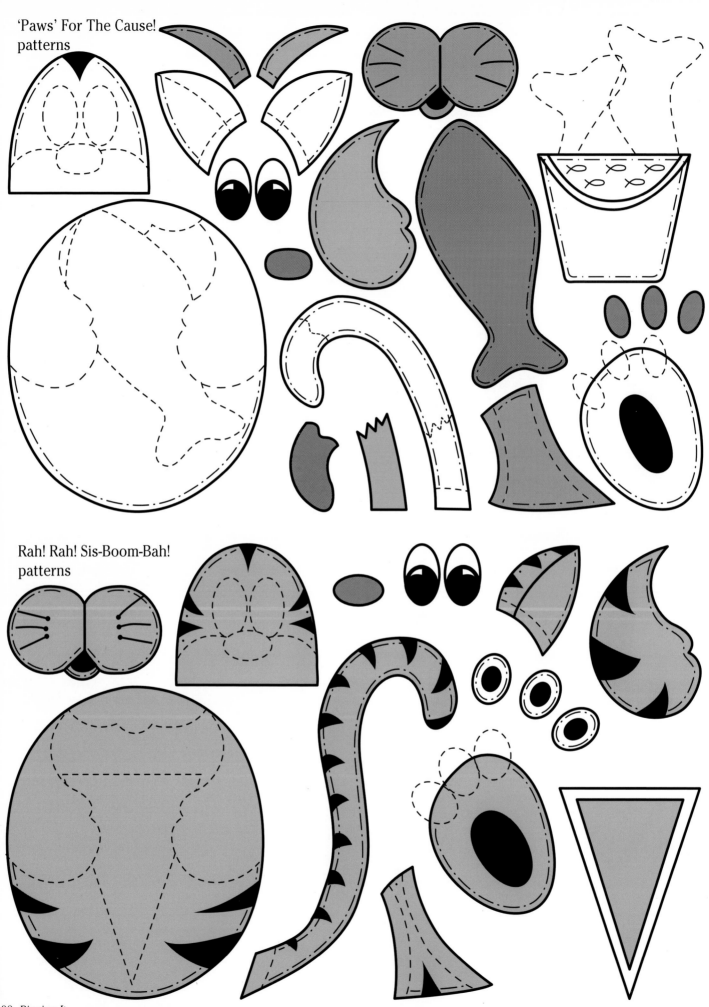

'Paws' For The Cause!
patterns

Rah! Rah! Sis-Boom-Bah!
patterns

'Paws' for The Cause!

Come on, kids! Stand still for just a couple of seconds! It's not every day that your team wins the soccer championship! And, look! There's a shot of your first-grader with his first A+ paper! It is the first in a long line of many, many more excellent achievements! And they all deserve a special page in the scrapbook!

Special Supplies: Papers - Cardstock (Olive, Beige, Brown, White, Orange & Black) and Keeping Memories Alive (Green plaid); Font: Signpost, on DJ Inkers Fontastic CD; 1/2" oval punch (toes).

Rah! Rah! Sis-Boom-Bah!

Boy! Was it ever cold at the homecoming game that year! The team thought we were cheering them on by stomping in the stands, but we were just trying to keep the blood flowing! No matter! Our team won!

Special Supplies: Papers - Cardstock (Black, Orange & White) and Paper Patch (Black check); Fonts: Flag - Varsity, a Printshop font, Title - CK Chunky, on Creating Keepsakes Volume II CD; 1/2" oval punch (eyes, nose, toes).

A Bear For All Seasons!

What a versatile bear this lady is! She appears here celebrating a patriot holiday.

Mother's Day Bear? Cut her a floral dress and pastel pinafore with a heart on the pocket. Replace the flag with an "I Love You, Mom!"sign.

A Birthday Bear? Create another dress and pinafore. Use a bunch of balloons in place of the flag.

Yule Tide Bear? Cut a Red dress, a Green pinafore and put a bow on her head. Use a "Deck the Halls" sign.

Papers - Cardstock (Dark Blue, Light Blue, Brown, Tan, White, Black, Silver, Red & Navy Blue), Keeping Memories Alive (Red check), Creating Memories (Blue star), Sonburn (Red check), 1/2" oval punch (eyes); 1/2" star punch.

Tina Lee

Tina, the "T" in TnC Scraps, the firm she started with her sister-in-law. With an Accounting degree from Oklahoma State University, she proves that anyone can be creative! Tina 'retired' in 1997 to stay home with her sons, Zachary and Nathan. An addiction to scrapbooking ensued, encouraged by her patient husband, Mike.

Catherine Martin

Catherine is the "C" in TnC Scraps. She majored in Art Education at Oklahoma State University and teaches public school. She, too, has two sons, Lane and Blake. Tina asked Catherine to draw designs for paper piecing and the creativity snowballed! Her proud husband, Mike, shares his own ideas for subjects.

Suppliers - Most craft and variety stores carry an excellent assortment of supplies. If you need something special, ask your local store to contact the following companies.

Papers - Frances Meyer, P.O. Box 3088, Savannah, GA 31402; **Keeping Memories Alive**, P.O. Box 728, Spanish Fork, UT 84660; **Paper Adventures**, P.O. Box 04393, Milwaukee, WI 53204; **Paper Patch**, P.O. Box 414 Riverton, VT 84065; **Provo Craft**, 285 E. 900 S., Provo, UT 84601; **Sonburn**, 3402 Wiley Post Road, Carrollton, Tx 75006

Tools - Provo Craft, 285 E. 900 S., Provo, UT 84601; **Fiskars**, 7811 W. Stewart Ave., Wausau, WI 54401; **Family Treasures**, 24922 Anza Dr., Unit D, Valencia, CA 91355; **AccuCut**, 1025 E. Dodge, Fremont, NE 69025; **Sailor Corp.**, 121 Bethea RD. #307, Fayetteville, GA 30214

Fonts - Creating Keepsakes, P.O. Box 469022, Escondido, CA 92046-9598l **D.J. Inkers**, P.O. Bos 1509, Sherwood, OR 97140; **Page Printables**, 3759 W. 2340 S., Suite D, Salt Lake City, UT 84120

MANY THANKS to my friends for their cheerful help and wonderful ideas!
Production Director - Kathy McMillan
Art Director - Jen Tennyson
Graphic Artist - Charlie Davis/Young
Editors - Wanda J. Little & Colleen Reigh
Photography - David & Donna Thomason